Hongyun Art

About this book and Hongyun Art

All of the stories and drawings you see are created by students of Hongyun Art.

Hongyun Art believes that art and creativity are intertwined in everyday life. We grow creativity and confidence by providing unique programs that challenge students to create ideas and then stand up and share their ideas with the world. We are constantly studying, growing, and advancing the art and science of creative education. After all, creativity is the root, the foundation, the spark that fuels our modern world.

www.XiaoDaVinci.com

Thanks to Audrey C. for her great rendition of our school name in a very creative form! We will feature this artwork in all of our books, on our school t-shirt, as well as on the outside of our school for at least one year! Great Job Audrey!

Contents

4

Teamwork
by Amber W. Age 5

The monkey, the wolf, and the giraffe are all good friends. They are the famous makers of the forest. One day, they found a little girl who was lost in the woods. The little girl didn't have a place to live but she was so nice and tried to help small animals. So the little makers decided to make a beautiful house for this little girl. They worked very hard and finally built a very nice tree house.

Then all the good friends moved nearby so that they can visit the little girl everyday. They then lived happily forever in the forest...

The end

Clean the Ocean
by Andre L. Age 7

One day, there was a group of people who wanted to clean the big ocean. Nick was the lead of the group. He was smart, nice, and brave. He was also experienced at cleaning the ocean. He drove the OCEAN-CLEANING boat, and vacuumed the trash, the recyclables, and the submerged cars. Suddenly, two bad guys came, and tried to throw more trash in the ocean. Nick and the team caught one bad guy and locked him in the boat. Then Nick threw a fake vacuum in the water and let it float to a really really far place. The other bad guy didn't like the vacuum, he thought that it was a real one. He chased it, and went away. Nick and the team completed the mission.

The end

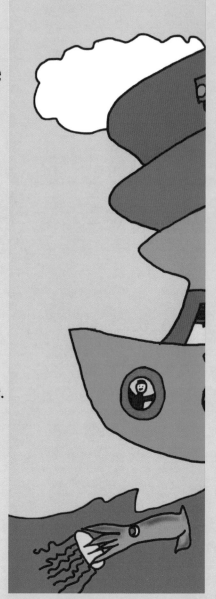

7

Rabbit's Tooth
by Annie W. Age 7

It was at night, the Rabbit was brushing her teeth when she felt a wiggling tooth. She knew it would come out very very very soon. She already lost one tooth and she made a tooth necklace with it. The Rabbit went to her bed and fell to sleep. Her friends, the hamsters all knew that the Rabbit's tooth would fall out. They told one another: "Rabbit's tooth will fall out soon....poor Rabbit. Let's help her!" They went to her bed. "If you be good, Rabbit, I will give you a sticker." said one hamster. Another one pulled the Rabbit's tooth out quickly. "Ouch!" cried the Rabbit. But she did not wake up. She was too tired. "Ouch!" Cried another little hamster. Believe or not, that little hamster's tooth fell out as well.

The end

My Teddy Bear Is Sick.
by Ariana J. Age 6

One day when my teddybear woke up she felt bad. The mice lived under her bed and tried to help. The mice gave her get well gifts too! But the clock rang and rang. One of the mice brought the medicine, her name is Lucy. The second mice brought the thermometer, his name was Tim.

The next morning, Fluffy bear felt even worse and then the mice tried to make Fluffy bear better. Then at night, she felt better and was able to play in the morning sun the whole day tomorrow.

The end

12

Fish School
by Audrey C. Age 8

Once, there were two fish, Goldie and Moldy. One miserable day, they went outside to play hoping to see their friends Hooves the horse and Waddle the swan. Of course, they weren't there. The friends were separated because of a hurricane earlier.

When the two fish went out, they found strange things. First, they discovered rare, shiny shells. Goldie thought she could make money or even add another section to their two section house. Moldy then discovered a ladder with two oxygen hats! Maybe they could find Hooves with that, or even Waddle!

Then they tried on the hats. The hats fit perfectly. They climbed on the slippery ladder carefully. When their heads went out of the water, they immediately spotted Waddle and Hooves!

The old friends talked for hours. Goldie bought a custom made ketch-up bottle with the shells. The bottle was decorated with even shinier shells and had a window at the top. With the hats and window, the friends could talk and play each other whenever they want to!

The end

Cookie Town
by Caleb C. Age 6

The cookie town is a small town which makes everything about cookies. A cookie truck is having it's ingredients filled up before it takes off to deliver delicious cookies with an option of ice-cream on top!

The end

Moon School
by Aidan L. Age 6

One day, a little boy went to the moon school. He saw a school bus flying. He climbed on the school bus. Then a rocket ship came. He got the rocket ship's wing and climbed on it. The rocket ship flew so fast and he fell down on the ground. He flew up again and catches the moon. Then he went back to the Earth. A space monkey saw a space restaurant and went inside. An alien came to catch the monkey. The Alien got the monkey and put him back to the Earth. Everybody on Earth wanted to go to the moon school and they all grabbed on the side of the moon school bus and ripped it. The moon was unhappy.

The end

Moon School
by Andrew P. Age 5

Today we drew moon school. I drew two moons that are at school. I drew a big elevator that is connected to Jupiter. The helicopter then crashed into there, but it did not break. A fish then came to the moon, and the stars were pointing to the big moon. A rocket got onto the comet so that it could go faster. A fish rocket went to the moon!

I was riding in a big ship. I saw two stars connected with a bridge. A star hopped and fell and the rocket ate it. I drew a bridge and it was connected in different colors. I went to the moon and I went down the elevator. I went to Jupiter. Then I went into the helicopter!

The end

Candy Monster
by Carolyn D. Age 7

Oh no! The Candy Monster is getting the candy!

First he grabbed a tree and started shaking candies off of it. And then he closed the Fruit shop and opened a candy shop!

He accidentally grabbed a baby banana. She had to go to the hospital. A cherry in an airplane flew up high and tried to spray water on the candy monster. It got sprayed back!

A cucumber said "Oh no!" A huge ice cream cone got spilled and toppled over the Candy Monster. Hooray!

The end

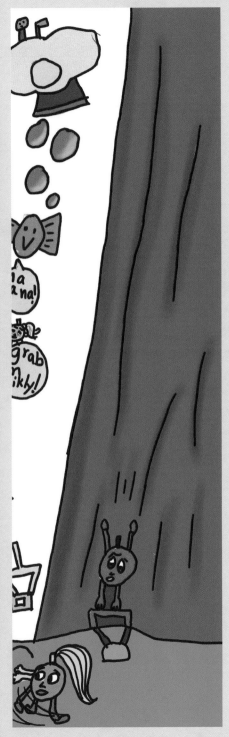

Candy Monster
by Carolyn Z. Age 6

One day in Fruit Town, an alien space ship from the Sugar Planet came by. Everybody in the Fruit Town was scared. The Aliens from Sugar Planet sucked up Fruit Town's Fruit Store using their magic light.

All of the apples tried to get away from the space ship. A tree from the Fruit Town and her daughter tried to save the apples. The mother tree used a pipe to suck the baby apples up to her branches. Her daughter shot magnet hooks to save the fruits from being sucked up to the Sugar Planet space ship. Also, a water bender created a water fall to stop the alien's magic light from sucking the apples.

The end

A Hot Day
by Helena H. Age 4

It is very hot.
The sun is shining a lot.
Everyone gets a balloon.
Everyone wants to eat ice-cream.
The flowers need water.

The end

25

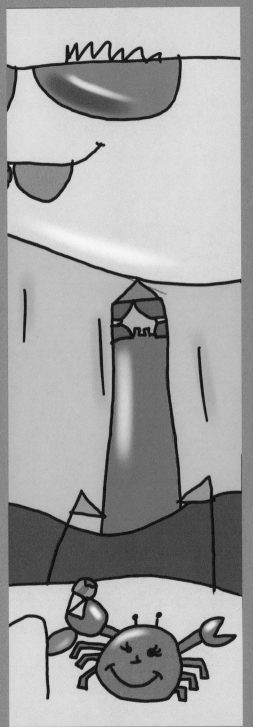

Summer
by Claire W. Age 5

It was so hot that day. Ms. Mermaid sat on a chair on the beach. Her water dog didn't want to come out of the water at all so he could avoid the heat. Even the Sun had sunglasses!

Now everybody got free ice-creams. Did you know that the little mouse had one too, but it is so tiny that nobody can see it!

Finally Ms.Mermaid got into the castle on the beach and met the owner who was a prince. They fell into love on that summer day and got married and had live happily for ever...

The end

Out of Place
by Audrey L. Age 6

There are two geese, one girl, and two boys who live in a house on the colored hills by a pond. But bad guys destroy their home! You can see their hands coming out of the house.

There were also three fish living in the pond. The bad guys messed up their home by putting a ladder between a rock and their home!

A girl who's diving is trying to get the ladder out. The sun also said, "what's going on?" One of the boys was hit by a bad guy, but it didn't hurt because it was a foam ball. The people who are there were looking around.

The end

28

Moon School
by Caroline C. Age 5

An adorable girl put on her beautiful red hair bow and got ready for the magnificent Moon school. She walked toward a yummy ice-cream cone and decided to take it to the Moon School as a snack. She was going to wait for the school bus by a cute and clever cherry tree.

Beep, beep, beep! Here came the smiley Moon School bus to pick up the girl. The bright lights were leading their way. Soon, the flying Moon School logo with a big Easter egg in front of the rainbow came to sight. It was wonderful that everyone wanted to go to the Moon School.

Two funny red and pink planets showed up. Even the bright green train joined the Moon School. More arrived in a big yellow balloon. An airplane flying all day transported many students to the Moon School.

Hooray! Hooray! Hooray! The fun started at Moon School!

The end

New Year Dinner
by Elizabeth Z. Age 5

Floating City
by Claire L. Age 7

The Helping City
by Elaine F. Age 7

Once upon a time, there was a big city on a boat. It was very nice weather. In the sky, a bird and a butterfly were flying. There were many balloons floating over the city. In the water, a girl was doing scuba diving. Two small ships, a little turtle and a lot of fishes surround her. A four-year boy was drowned when he went swimming. The helping city pulled him up and rescued him!

The end

Fish City
by Emily C. Age 8

Summer Cool Down
by Gloria P. Age 5

Self Portrait
by Emily S. Age 7

I am Emily. I am seven and a half years old. I live with my dad, mom, and my little sister Melody. I like doing gymnastics the best. The fun part is jumping on the trampoline and hanging on the bars. In my day, I like painting a lot. One of my favorite thing is drawing for "Doodle for Google". My best interest is in animals. My favorite animals are rabbits and sea animals. I went to Sea World and saw dolphins and Shamus. They were very active and friendly. Whenever I have time I like to read. My favorite book is Sam The Stolen Puppy. I also like to eat many different fruit. My favorite fruit is cherries. I make many kinds of cookies with my dad. Chocolate chip cookie is my favorite. I am always curious and eager to learn!

The end

Healthy Village War
by Hannah L. Age 8

One sunny day in the Healthy Village, something weird happened. There was a giant rumble, then theHealthy Village suddenly became JunkFood Land! The villagers then realized that the Junks were trying to destroy the village!

The evil Gingerbread Master came in and smooshed as many fruits as he could. The Skittles, Chocolate, and Candy Cane Eaters came in and started munching apples. An ice cream shouted "Eat us not healthy food!" Meanwhile, a lollipop squished juice from an apple and now, all was chaos!

Suddenly a blue waterfall from the clouds washed out all the tiny candies. In Apple school, the teacher was shouting, "Save them! Save them! Save them!" The little apples had no idea what was going on and one cried "don't kill us" and another said "help us!" The war ended three days later and it was so messy. The Junks were defeated and they had learned a lesson. Junks are not good for people.

The end

41

Team Work
by Winston X. Age 5

All of the people want to build a tree house. The animals want to help!

The bird is bringing some paint to the rooftop. The elephant is making a river outside so that they can swim in. The cat is thinking about what he should do. Even the car is helping them.

Some people are busy pouring the water from the well and some are hiding money for them to use later. One person is trying to make a ladder for the tree house. And one person is cheering for the person that is carring a heavy bucket of water up the tree house.

The end

Candy Attack
by Olive T. Age 7

Candy Store
by Jaleyna L Age 8

Team Work
by Tanisha A. Age 5

My picture is about "teamwork."

The bird is cleaning the tree-house. The sunflower is watering the other flowers. The rock is supporting the tree-house. The tree is putting bows on the tree-house. The truck is delivering a package to the boy. The boy is hanging clothes on the clothes line.

The end

Team Work
by Janet L. Age 7

Once upon a time, there were five animals who lived together in a palace: dog, cat, horse, bunny, and Fire, the lady bug.

The animals came to the rainbow birthday party. They were doing what they could to make a cake. Dog and cat were stirring the cream. Horse scooped the cream. Ladybug put decorations. Bunny put on a cherry. Rainbow put sprinkles on the cake. At last, the cake was ready! It was all team work!

The end

Team Work
by Joshua L. Age 7

Candy attack
Kaelynn T. Age 7

52

Fish School
by Mai O. Age 7

In the deep, blue ocean, at the bottom of a sea, no one knew there was a school for fish. Even starfish and whales came to the school!

The school is for kindergarten to 3rd grade. Some beautiful corals and seaweeds are surrounding the school. Sometimes, even a few hermit crabs come to the school. And, the cars have fins instead of tires, but the shape is same as a normal car.

When the sun is shining into the water, it is very, very pretty in the ocean. And luckily, today was the day for the easter egg hunt (that was really real for me, Mai)!! And the real fun tomorrow is an easter egg competition! The rules are to decorate a boiled egg and their parents can also enter the competition. Each fish from every class can get a medal and a treat!

Who will win from each class......??

The end

Cookie Town
by Niyatee J. Age 6

One day in cookie town, there was the 100th anniversary. The president was so excited the couldn't wait to see the bakery's cookies! But he saw his friend from the real world so he stood on the windows.

The end

Out of Place
by Mai O. Age 7

Fish Home
Takehide Age 12

Super Car
by Raymond T. Age 6

Tom and Tim love racing cars. They once built a super car and they were very excited that they would go racing the coming summer.

When the day came, Tom and Tim wore their cleanest shirts ever! The race started at 3:25pm and they need to run 609 laps. It was a long race, but it wouldn't be boring because they had a super car and they could do a lot of things on it.

Tom was reading his ABC book. It was actually a very thick dictionary. Tim was drinking his favorite juice while watching the super car playing arch and arrows. It felt so good to have some icy juice during the hot summer. The super car's name is 4x4. He was busy during the race. He need to change wheels from time to time. He also need to wave his hands to please the cheering audience. But he still got time to play arch and arrows, and he was so good at it.

Tom and Tim were sure that they would win. After 609 laps, they were actually 2nd place! Rim and Ram were 1st. Percy and Pax were 3rd. They were all winners! Tom and Tim were very happy! They decided to come back with their super car 4x4 again next year so they will be better at it.

The end

Candy attack
by Michael C. Age 7

Summer Cooldown
by Irene Y. Age 6

Ice Cream for Fish
by Deelia W. Age 7

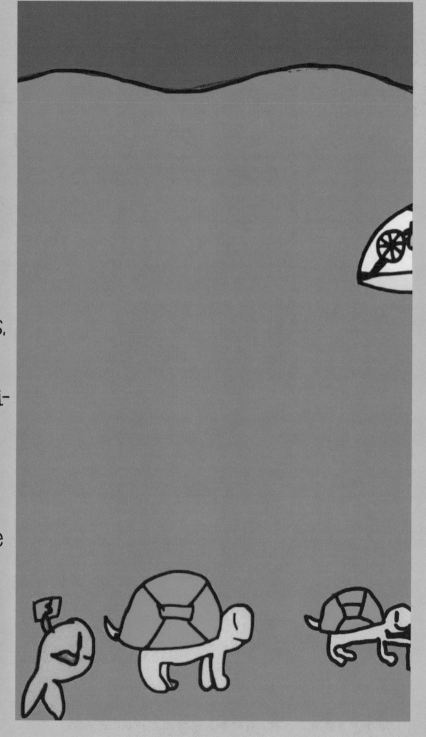

On a hot summer day, under the warm sea, there was an ice cream shop. Everyone went there when they heard about it. It was crowded with animals, not only because the ice cream was tasty, but also the air conditioning made it very cool inside the shop. Other foods in the ice cream shop were very tasty and smelled fresh, too. Everyone enjoyed it!

The end

63

64

Future Artsit
by
Jaleyna L.
Age 8

Music Party
by Audrey C. Age 8

Boom - de - Boom - de - Boom,
Sang all the instrument friends.
Doom - la - Boom - la - Doom,
Their sound cheerfully fills the room!

"Let's dance!"
Shouted the ErHu while giving a
glance.
"Don't let the music stop,
Or else our spirits will drop!"

"Ding - Ding!"
The cymbal twins sing,
"This is so fun!
Look how much happiness this will
bring!"

"Pluck. Pluck. Pluck!"
Plucked the PiPa full of luck.
"Let the joy spread."
He happily said.
"Don't just sit there like a pile of
muck!"

"Whoo - Whoo - Whoooo!"
Blew the DiZi, too.
He huffed and puffed.
And finally his music got fluffed.
"This is hard, but fun." He huffed.

"Hit. Hit. Hit!"
Cried the drum, doing a split.
"I keep the tempo well.
I'm as good as a bell!"

The six friends played and played.
The audience listened in the shade.
When they finished, it was far past
sundown.
But no one was ready for their night
gown.
They clapped and cried. "We want
more!
Music is fun!"

Candy Attack!
by Jennifer S. Age 8

And that's it for now!

We hope you enjoyed this book

We have several more books created by our students on the way!

Please check our website www.XiaoDaVinci.com often for more information